I0087904

Friendly Leadership

Humanely Influencing Others

Donn Weinholtz

FMS
Full Media Services
fullmediaservices.com

Contents

Library of Congress Number:
TXu002271605

E-Book ISBN: 978-1-7336152-8-0
Print ISBN: 978-1-7336152-7-3

Definition

Friendly Leadership: *Humanely influencing others to seek positive, mutually rewarding outcomes.*

There are many definitions of leadership and some authors devote pages to parsing the differences among them. Instead of doing so, I am stipulating the brief definition shown above. It is clear and simple, and it contains a moral component often missing in leadership definitions. It emphasizes humane behavior and mutually beneficial results; thus, logically ruling out criminal activities, as well as legal, but crass, self-interest. Leadership can be examined from an amoral perspective, as did Machiavelli, but I won't be doing so, here.

Also, "to seek" indicates goal–oriented behavior, without stipulating success. One can lead well, but still fail. Success often depends on the resources and obstacles encountered along the way, variables perhaps well beyond a leader's control. It is important to acknowledge that serendipity often plays a critical role in group achievement.

Prologue

We spend much of our time living, working and playing with others in small groups and in larger organizations. Frequently, we are not mindful of group efficiency and effectiveness; but at times they are very important to us. This brief volume focuses on those times that group and organizational effectiveness are our primary concerns.

The content is substantially shaped by my perspectives as a liberal Quaker, yet much here is secular in nature. Although Quaker and non-Quaker illustrations are sprinkled throughout, there are no references to vital spiritual notions such as "the Divine" or "the Light within." Also, there are no references to notable Friends such as George Fox, Margaret Fell, William Penn, Susan B. Anthony, Elise Boulding, Bayard Rustin or others. So, why bother highlighting the Quaker orientation?

First, my views are so deeply influenced by Quaker testimonies – particularly peace, integrity, community, and equality – that frank acknowledgement is warranted. Second, the skills emphasized here can be valuable tools for anyone, but they are especially well suited for clerks of Quaker committees, a Meeting clerk, and an entire Meeting's membership. Among Quakers, in particular, emergent leadership of Meeting members is as important as the leadership exhibited by the clerks. Nevertheless, Quakers are sometimes ambivalent about discussing leadership due to the inherent tension between individual assertiveness and achieving "unity" in decision-making. I believe that Friends might benefit from informed discussions about leadership, and this slim volume might help to promote such exchanges.

Also, Quakers spend most of their time operating in the secular world, rather than among Friends. The challenge of practicing Quaker values in a world often adhering to standards contrary to those advocated by Friends can be difficult. The leadership behaviors described here may prove helpful when navigating the world around us.

Still, having laid out this case for Quaker-oriented leadership, I recognize that there is already so much leadership literature out there that it's reasonable to ask, "Why add this booklet to the collection?" The answer is that this is the brief, common sense guide that I sought for many years, but never found. It is intentionally not exhaustive. Assuming that "less is more," I've boiled a great deal of material down to a few essential insights based on a handful of lessons learned throughout my adult life. I've gathered these insights for you, trying to avoid much of the cumbersome jargon and extraneous detail often found in leadership books. Also, I've provided illustrations, some simple others more complex, of leadership behaviors from both Quaker and secular settings. And I've included an Appendix focused on facilitating Zoom meetings, to begin to address new leadership challenges initiated by the COVID pandemic. So, in spite of its Quaker orientation, this volume should be useful for anyone interested in group and leadership dynamics. I'll be pleased if people other than Friends find it helpful.

Finally, the recommendations here come with no guarantees because there are no foolproof leadership recipes that always yield immediate, impressive, successes. Although the suggestions are solid, life is so complicated that no leadership advice can be counted on to always ensure desired results. The most that any of us can do is to try to hone our leadership skills as opportunities arise. Sometimes we will succeed handsomely, and other times we will come up short, hopefully learning from our setbacks.

Introduction

"The servant-leader...wants to serve, to serve first, as opposed to, wanting power, influence, fame, or wealth."
Robert Greenleaf

Robert Greenleaf's (2002) book, *Servant Leadership: A Journey into the Nature of Legitimate Power & Greatness* is a fine place to begin a Quaker-oriented, Friendly leadership discussion. A "convinced" Friend, Greenleaf focused on skills important for the leaders of large institutions, such as the trustees of colleges and seminaries, as well as for various historical figures. Surprisingly, he only made passing reference to their importance in everyday, smaller groups. Also, he made no mention at all regarding how servant leadership skills describe the behaviors of an effective Quaker clerk.

Greenleaf's neglect of small groups was not unusual. Academic discussions of leadership frequently focus upon historic figures operating on a grand stage, often to the exclusion of the less dramatic leadership situations in everyday life. Joan of Arc, Abraham Lincoln, Andrew Carnegie, Winston Churchill, Margaret Thatcher, Martin Luther King, Mahatma Gandhi, Golda Meir, Mother Theresa, Nelson Mandela, Angela Merkel, Steve Jobs, Sheryl Sandberg, Barack Obama and Bill Gates are among the many whose leadership skills are regularly scrutinized. However, few individuals ever obtain such stature. The overwhelming majority of us function beneath the radar of historians and the media.

Still, effective leadership practices are relevant to us all. We all find ourselves in situations where leadership - either our own or that of others - directly impacts the quality of our lives. Sometimes, thoughtful leaders serve us well; and just as frequently, ineffective leaders exasperate and frustrate us.

As cited on the *The Robert K. Greanleaf Center for Servant Leadership* website (http://www.greenleaf.org), the ten core Servant Leadership skills are:

1. **Listening** - *Traditionally, leaders have been valued for their communication and decision-making skills. Servant-leaders must reinforce these important skills by making a deep commitment to listening intently to others. Servant-leaders seek to identify and clarify the will of a group. They seek to listen receptively to what is being said (and not said). Listening also encompasses getting in touch with one's inner voice, and seeking to understand what one's body, spirit, and mind are communicating.*
2. **Empathy** - *Servant-leaders strive to understand and empathize with others. People need to be accepted and recognized for their special and unique spirit. One must assume the good intentions of coworkers and not reject them as people, even when forced to reject their behavior or performance.*
3. **Healing** - *Learning to heal is a powerful force for transformation and integration. One of the great strengths of servant-leadership is the potential for healing one's self and others. In "The Servant as Leader", Greenleaf writes, "There is something subtle communicated to one who is being served and led if, implicit in the compact between the servant-leader and led is the understanding that the search for wholeness is something that they have."*

4. **Awareness** - *General awareness, and especially self-awareness, strengthens the servant-leader. Making a commitment to foster awareness can be scary--one never knows that one may discover! As Greenleaf observed, "Awareness is not a giver of solace - it's just the opposite. It disturbs. They are not seekers of solace. They have their own inner security.*
5. **Persuasion** - *Servant-leaders rely on persuasion, rather than positional authority in making decisions. Servant-leaders seek to convince others, rather than coerce compliance. This particular element offers one of the clearest distinctions between the traditional authoritarian model and that of servant-leadership. The servant-leader is effective at building consensus within groups.*
6. **Conceptualization** - *Servant-leaders seek to nurture their abilities to "dream great dreams." The ability to look at a problem (or an organization) from a conceptualizing perspective means that one must think beyond day-to-day realities. Servant-leaders must seek a delicate balance between conceptualization and day-to-day focus.*
7. **Foresight** - *Foresight is a characteristic that enables servant-leaders to understand lessons from the past, the realities of the present, and the likely consequence of a decision in the future. It is deeply rooted in the intuitive mind.* ***Foresight*** *and the previously mentioned* ***conceptualization*** *merge in a leader's overall* ***vision,*** *the ability to imagine the future in novel and productive ways and a key characteristic to fulfilling the roles that follow.*
8. **Stewardship** - *Greenleaf's view of all institutions was one in which CEO's, staff, directors, and trustees all play significant roles in holding their institutions in trust for the great good of society.*

9. **Commitment to the Growth of People** - *Servant-leaders believe that people have an intrinsic value beyond their tangible contributions as workers. As such, servant-leaders are deeply committed to a personal, professional, and spiritual growth of each and every individual within the organization.*
10. **Building Community** - *Servant-leaders are aware that the shift from local communities to large institutions as the primary shaper of human lives has changed our perceptions and has caused a feeling of loss. Servant-leaders seek to identify a means for building community among those who work within a given institution. In particular, the leader's ability to foster development of a* ***shared vision*** *plays a key role in a group's overall satisfaction and success.*

This is a daunting set of responsibilities, and fulfilling these roles requires patience, skill and faith in one's self and one's fellow group members. All of us would benefit from growth in each of the areas. To address that need, the recommendations that follow are intended to facilitate relevant personal development. Again, this volume is aimed primarily, with the exception of the complex Catalytic Leadership approach appearing near the end, at the micro-level leadership that we all encounter on a daily basis. The simplest form of such leading is found in dyads, groups consisting of only two people. It also occurs in small groups of friends, families, and work teams within organizations, the context of much of our lives. Consistent with the literature on small group dynamics, I've made no attempt to delve into the challenges confronting leaders of more complex systems, such as organization financial and strategic management. I have thoughts on such matters, but they are not my real area of expertise and are better left to those writing other publications.

Chapter 1

Communication Skills

> *"Don't assume, because you are intelligent, able, and well-motivated, that you are open to communication, that you know how to listen."*
>
> Robert Greeenleaf

Human groups frequently experience confusion and conflict. In spite of our good intentions, we are prone to miscommunication and we suffer the consequences. Also, we often have dramatically different priorities and motives, causing us to run afoul of each other.

Effective leaders may be able to minimize the negative impacts of these problems and channel group energy towards achieving positive goals. As Greenleaf (2002) observed, doing so requires skillful communication. Indeed, effective communication is the heart of good leadership.

Four communication skills that leaders should develop are: 1) active listening; 2) assertiveness 3) win-win problem solving - sometimes called no-lose negotiation; and 4) being clear and concise. The first three are explained in detail by Thomas Gordon (2001) in his book, *Leadership Effectiveness Training*, from which I'll be drawing heavily. The fourth is too often glossed over or missing from leadership texts; but it deserves focused attention.

Skill development involves proceeding through distinct learning stages**.** As shown below, before you start attempting to develop new skills, you will probably be *unconsciously unskilled;* in other words, unaware of the fact that you don't possess the skill. You may even be unaware that the skill exists at all. This stage, as well as those that follow, are presented in Figure 1.

Learning Stages:

1. **Unconsciously Skilled**
2. **Consciously Skilled**
3. **Consciously Unskilled**
4. **Unconsciously Unskilled**

Figure 1. Learning Stages Adams, Linda. https://www.gordontraining.com/free-workplace-articles/learning-a-new-skill-is-easier-said-than-done/ Retrieved April 19, 2019.

As you start working on developing a skill, such as listening, you will become *consciously unskilled* , meaning that you will be aware that you haven't mastered the skill; and you will feel awkward, perhaps like you felt when you first tried to ride a bicycle. With continued practice, however, you will soon become *consciously skilled***,** meaning that you will be able to selectively apply the skill when you recognize situations calling for it. This is certainly a higher stage of development, but it is not as sophisticated as you can get. What you want to strive for is being *unconsciously skilled***,** which occurs when you are so capable of using the skill that it becomes a normal part of your behavioral repertoire and you use it automatically in appropriate situations. With this information in mind, let's examine the most fundamental and essential communication skill, *Active Listening*.

Active Listening

One of the reasons that there is so much confusion and conflict in the world is that we often do a poor job of listening to each other. Too frequently, poor listening creates tense situations and makes already tense situations worse. Since leaders are only human, they sometimes fall short in this regard, and can benefit greatly by further developing their communication skills. (Confession: As I write these words, I am reminded that, in spite of years of thought and listening practice, I still sometimes contribute to downward communication spirals because I do not listen well enough.)

There are many common *listening errors* that undermine effective communication, especially in heated situations involving people who "push each others' buttons" (for example between family members who know those buttons best.) As highlighted below, we may *over listen* (jump to conclusions or read too much into what another has said) or we may err in the other direction and *under listen* by not paying sufficient attention to what the other person is saying, thereby missing the deeper meaning. When *over listening*, we may make the mistake of trying to quickly solve others' problems for them; and since we don't hear all that others have said, we may cause them to become frustrated or angry. When we *under listen*, we may communicate to others that we don't really care about their problems, perceptions, feelings or opinions. This may also result in frustration or anger, since the person was merely hoping for someone to lend a friendly ear.

Common Listening Errors

Over Listening	Under Listening
Overshooting	Undershooting
Adding	Omitting
Rushing	Lagging
Analyzing	Parroting

Figure 2: Common Listening Errors Adams, Michelle. https://www.gordontraining.com/leadership/improve-active-listening-avoiding-common-errors/ Retrieved April 18, 2019.

Several of the most common *over listening* errors and *under listening* errors are shown above. Sometimes we combine these listening errors with the common communication *roadblocks* shown below, making others feel uncomfortable and defensive.

Communication Roadblocks

Solutions	Ordering, Threatening, Moralizing, Advising, Lecturing
Judgements	Blaming, Labeling, Analyzing
Discounts	Praising, Reassuring
Questions	Probing
Avoidances	Reassuring

Figure 3: Communication Roadblocks Gordon, T. *Leader Effectiveness Training*. Pedigree Books, 2001.

Of course, rather than *over listening, under listening*, and introducing communications *roadblocks*; it is best to carefully attend to others' messages. This is especially true in situations where there is conflict or the potential for conflict. A highly effective approach to listening – appropriate for leaders in many situations - is *active listening*. Indeed, active listening may be the most important of all *Friendly Leadership* behaviors. The active listening steps are illustrated below, in a case showing the language the clerk of a Quaker meeting might use in response to the concerns expressed by a frustrated member of the meeting.

Active Listening Case 1: *The Hurried Quaker Business Meeting*

Acknowledging Problem Ownership: *"You seem...*

Reflecting Emotion or Feeling: *distressed about...*

Describing the Facts: *...us having rushed to a decision about how to spend the remainder of the Peace and Social Concerns budget."*

(Note: This case and the one that follows are further developed to include I-messages and Win-win Problem Solving in the next several pages.)

This second case illustrates a classroom teacher applying active listening in a conversation with a student who is visibly unhappy after having gotten back his Statistics test.

Active Listening Case 2: *The Statistics Test*

Acknowledging Problem Ownership: *"You appear...*
Reflecting Emotion or Feeling: *to be pretty upset...*
Describing the Facts: *about your score on the test."*

The great strength of *active listening* is that it increases the chances of truly hearing what others are saying; including their deeper meanings; while defusing some of the emotional intensity frequently accompanying difficult encounters. Often, people will not initially reveal what is troubling them; either because they may not yet know themselves and they need to talk in order to figure out what is upsetting them, or because they do not want to share their deeper concerns until they sense that they are in a trusting environment. *Active listening* is a valuable skill in creating an atmosphere where authentic communication can take place, whether it is in a work team trying to figure out novel solutions to particular problems or a one-on-one session with an employee, colleague or family member who is experiencing job-related or personal problems.

A critical aspect of active listening is doing so comfortably; without appearing contrived or patronizing. As indicated earlier, this involves becoming *unconsciously skilled.* By deeply embedding the behavior into your skill set through persistently working on becoming a better listener, the benefits will become apparent.

Assertiveness Skills: *I – Messages*

Although active listening is the foundational skill upon which effective communication and conflict resolution efforts are based, it alone is insufficient to provide clarity and prevent or resolve many conflicts. Frequently, it is necessary for individuals who are either disagreeing with each other, or negotiating with each other, to express their own positions in a candid, assertive and non-threatening manner. A communication skill well suited for this purpose is the I- message. The steps involved in delivering I-Messages are shown immediately below. They are followed first by a continuation of the case that already provided of a Quaker clerk responding to a frustrated committee member regarding a budget decision; then by a second illustration building on the case of the teacher/student interaction regarding the student's Statistics test performance. (Note: All of the skills identified below, for both I-Messages and Win-Win Problem Solving are, adapted from Gordon, T. *Leader Effectiveness Training*. Pedigree Books, 2001.)

I- Messages

I feel / need / appreciate: *State the feeling.*
When: *Describe the situation or behavior resulting in the feeling.*
Because: *Without blaming others, explain the basis of your feelings.*
Therefore: *If possible, explain what you would like to see happen.*

I-Message Case 1: *The Hurried Quaker Business Meeting (continued)*

I feel / need / appreciate: I understand your frustration.
When: We did rush to a decision towards the close of Business Meeting when the number of Friends remaining was small, and you could no longer be present.

Because: I realize that your concerns were not heard.

Therefore: So, I will send out a message to all of the Friends on the Meeting listserv to see if we can suspend our decision on the Peace and Social Concerns budget and resume our discernment at a "called meeting" following worship next Sunday.

I-Message Case 2: *The Statistics Test (continued)*

I feel / need / appreciate: "I'm distressed too...

When: I really want to teach this material well, and it frustrates me when I realize that students are struggling with it;

Because: especially because I struggled with Statistics the first time that I took it, I know what you are feeling.

Therefore: So, I am hoping that you'll learn from the comments I provided you on your test, and that you'll do much better on the retest. Also, as a class, we can generate some strategies that that I can use to improve my instruction and help everyone do better.

As with developing active listening skill, learning how to successfully use I-Messages does not come naturally or easily. It must be consciously practiced, and it will feel awkward at first. In order to learn the skill, it is helpful to remember the key characteristics of I-messages, listed below.

. . .

I- Messages are:

- **Self-Disclosing**
- **Direct**
- **Clear**
- **Authentic**

Over time, you will find that using **I-messages** in combination with **active listening** yields many positive results, including:

Benefits of I-Messages

- **People's Needs Get Met**
- **You Develop a Strengthened Sense of Self**
- **You are Better Understood by Others**
- **It Helps Prevent Conflicts**

Win-Win Problem Solving

As previously indicated, active listening and I-messages are powerful communication skills when used alone or in combination. A third critical skill is *Win-Win Problem Solving***.** As the name indicates, the goal of this approach is to get the participating parties to collaborate on finding mutually agreeable solutions to the problems confronting them. Working together is essential, as it provides participating parties with the sense of ownership necessary to assure successful implementation of whatever solutions are adopted. Without this "buy-in" people are likely to participate unenthusiastically, or not at all. Even worse, they may work to sabotage solutions that they feel were forced upon them.

The six steps involved in Win / Win problem solving are:

1. **Identify the Problem**
2. **Identify the Feelings**
3. **Brainstorm Solutions**
4. **Choose a Solution**
5. **Agree to Act.**
6. **Evaluate the Solution**

Below, our two case studies proceed to their conclusions.

Win-Win Problem Solving Case 1: *The Hurried Quaker Business Meeting*

Building on the *Peace and Social Concerns* budget illustration presented previously, a "called" meeting is held. At the meeting, the clerk explains, as she had presumably done in the listserv email, that time constraints had limited the opportunity for Friends to express a full range of options regarding how the remainder of the budget might be spent, leaving some Friends exasperated (Steps *1 & 2*.) She then allows some time for Friends to share their feelings - such as frustration and anger, or perhaps satisfaction with the prior meeting's decision and resulting anxiousness to quickly move forward - to ensure that their needs and values are understood. Following this period of "clearing the air," she asks the person whose original complaint had resulted in the "called" meeting to express his preferences and invites others (some of whom were not at the original Business Meeting) to share their views. By doing so, a substantial list of options, addressing the needs and values of those present, is generated and written down by the recording clerk (Step 3.) From this list, the Meeting members and attenders then come to unity on ways that they can allocate the budget (Step 4), as well as develop plans for dispersing the funds (Step 5.) Finally, they agree to revisit these spending priorities during the following year's budget discussions, making decisions about renewal and reallocation based on the perceived effectiveness of the initial allocations (Step 6.)

. . .

Win-Win Problem Solving Case 2: *The Statistics Test*

In addition to providing students who performed poorly on the Statistics test an opportunity to take a retest, the teacher previously committed to facilitating a class discussion dedicated to soliciting students' ideas regarding instructional strategies that she might implement in order to help the class better learn Statistics. Such a discussion offers the opportunity for a Win-Win solution. It begins with the teacher explaining to the class that Statistics is a difficult class to teach, as well as a difficult subject to learn, and that she, along with a portion of the students, can get very frustrated with the process (Steps 1 & 2.) After allowing the students an opportunity to share their feelings – such as their fear, anxiety and frustration -the teacher leads an exercise where, on the chalk board, she lists students' suggestions for improving the teaching/learning process (Step 3.) By consensus, or vote if it is not a Quaker school, the class then chooses 2 or 3 strategies for the teacher to adopt, and the teacher commits to giving them a try (Steps 4 & 5.) Finally, based on future test results and student evaluations the teacher and class assess the effectiveness of the plan (Step 6.)

Notice that both cases involve a multi-step process, so there are plenty of opportunities for things to become highly complicated and for discussions to derail. Consequently, active listening and I-messages are important throughout. Applying each of these skills during collaborative problem solving maximizes the chances of staying on course, rather than getting bogged down in distracting, side disputes.

Also, it is important to not be overly rigid when following the steps in the sequence shown above. For example, while in the middle of generating solutions, the deeper nature of a problem may become clear and may require adjusting to that fact in mid-course. Also, it is helpful to adopt language with which you are comfortable, rather than the words stipulated by the model. For example, you might say "Let's make sure that everyone gets a chance to share their suggestions regarding how we might proceed;" rather than "It's time to brainstorm a set of solutions."

Being Clear and Concise

To lead effectively and humanely it's important not to perplex people with confusing messages, or frustrate them by taking up too much of their time by excessively talking at them or by sending them long, complicated emails. Clarity and precision are important skills to hone. They can prevent so many problems.

There certainly are exceptions. Bill Clinton is a prime example of someone who often spoke well beyond desirable limits. (Charisma provides some people a pass.) But we shouldn't try to emulate such role models. It's important to avoid becoming seduced by the sounds of our own voices, the compelling importance of our messages, and our ability to dominate, just because our position allows it.

Communicating clearly and concisely comes more easily to some, than to others. Thoughtful reflection on how to do so is time well spent, and regularly applying a few smart strategies can be especially helpful. For example, having a trusted colleague or friend review written communications can be very beneficial for editing out extraneous words or sentences, as well as gaining insight into points that need to be amplified or clarified. Also, mentally boiling down oral presentations to the few most essential points can prevent long-windedness. As with the other types of communication, the goal is to develop the skills over time, so that they become reflexive, natural behaviors. Since most of us are not gifted communicators, this can only be accomplished by practice, practice, practice.

Implicit Bias

My colleague, Laura Rediehs, Professor of Philosophy at St. Lawrence University, read an early draft of this volume, and offered the following insight.

As I read the part on active listening, I thought of another factor that might be worth mentioning: another common listening error has to do with gender, but may well affect minorities as well: a tendency that some have to not hear the contributions made by women or minorities. Women, for example, have the common experience of saying things in meetings that no one seems to acknowledge or value until, several comments later, a white male makes a similar comment and then everyone admires its wisdom. (This is surprisingly so common that women now often team up to watch for these moments so that when the moment comes that a man echoes the comment a woman had previously made, another woman then credits the original woman for having made that very comment a few moments ago!)....Both male and female leaders can inadvertently make this mistake....Even well-intentioned people can succumb to implicit biases of not taking certain voices seriously (e.g., women, minorities, or specific individuals one may have previously had tensions with), and it is easy for the leader or an entire group to inadvertently under-listen to such people.

So, how are leaders to deal with these blind spots, the unconscious biases of which they're not even aware, that can easily result in **micro-aggressions** that derail effective group collaboration by diminishing and suppressing the important voices and contributions of some group members? This is a particularly thorny issue tied, not just to universal human frailty, but also to longstanding conditions of male dominance and white privilege. Fortunately, in the era of the *Me Too* and *Black Lives Matter* movements, as Laura's example above illustrates, emboldened females and people of color are less likely to let such behavior pass unchallenged. When such challenges occur within groups, the "leader" must strive to help facilitate productive discussion by listening even more intently and accepting constructive criticism, rather than retreating into defensive denial.

This, of course, is not easy. As the case below illustrates, substantial tension is likely to arise; but if the problems can be transcended, important individual and group growth can occur.

. . .

Inter-racial Communication Case Study: *A Perceived Micro-Aggression*

Nearly thirty years ago, I was participating in a collaborative, mixed-gender and mixed-racial leadership group of mid-level administrators working to create a leadership institute for parents in the Hartford, Connecticut school system. This team effort eventually proved quite successful, but the group's diversity presented some challenges.

For example, during a working dinner meeting early in the group's development, Miguel, a psychiatrist and manager within the city's health department was describing the daily frustrations experienced by economically deprived parents of color. Miguel was originally from South America. He had been living in the United States for over a decade. The stories he told were compelling, detailing the harsh realities of people's day-to-day lives. Listening to him, I was deeply moved by the pain he described. I felt great sympathy.

However, my facial expression – I winced – conveyed something altogether different to Miguel. Seeing a middle-aged white man, steeped in privilege, with a contorted look on his face; based on so much prior experience, Miguel perceived a micro-aggression. His affect swiftly and dramatically changed. He flashed me an angry look, and he demanded to know how I could be so dismissive. Taken aback, I was both shocked and hurt. How could Miguel, who I both liked and respected, see me in this light? How were we going to resolve this sudden, unexpected issue?

Fortunately, we were able to resolve the matter, as several factors worked in our favor. First, Miguel, the trained psychiatrist, was a remarkably good listener. Second, the encounter occurred within a group of caring witnesses. Third, due to various prior experiences I was well aware of the intercultural miscommunications that can easily occur across ethnic and racial groups. Thus, my immediate reaction was not to fight back, but rather hear Miguel out, and sincerely explain what I was feeling.

Thankfully, Miguel accepted my explanation and offered me a sincere apology, saying he hoped that I could understand what had triggered his response. Indeed, I could understand, and we were able to work together effectively collaborating from that moment on. In fact, our relationship was strengthened by the encounter.

Many crossed communications due to implicit bias, or perceived implicit bias, are far more difficult to resolve than the one described here. One critical problem is simply getting such issues surfaced for discussion and possible resolution. Lisa Graustein (2020) recently described a promising "experiment" being implemented within New England Yearly Meeting of Friends. It involves appointing people to "observe, name, and reflect back...long-standing, unseen patterns and practices that result in...complicity in oppression." Clearly, such work, while extremely important, is very delicate. However, when people of good will practice effective communication skills and persist in their efforts to find common ground, remarkable healing and growth can occur.

Of course, it is desirable, if possible, to prevent unnecessary conflicts from occurring in the first place. The introductory section to the following chapter presents steps that leaders can take to promote healthy diversity, equity and inclusion.

Chapter 2

Group Dynamics

"The group dynamic can bring synergy, or tear things apart."
Margaret Bau

Any group leader is well served by a firm grasp of group dynamics, the behavioral patterns underlying human interactions. The research on small group dynamics is vast, so I will only briefly address some key essentials, here. Because inter-racial and inter-cultural communication are increasingly affecting group interactions, I start by further exploring some of the group diversity issues introduced at the conclusion of the last chapter.

Group Diversity, Equity and Inclusion

Because most of the materials cited throughout this volume were produced in a white, male and heterosexual dominated, academic milieu, they do not address the potential oppression of female, LGBTQ+, racial minority, and disabled members within groups. As the previous chapter's section on *Implicit Bias* indicates, oppressive micro-aggressions are generally not even apparent to majority group members, while they are compellingly real and painful for minority group members. Furthermore, it is increasingly apparent that *diversity* (as reflected in Guilford College's Diversity Statement https://www.guilford.edu/who-we-are/office-diversity-equity-and-inclusion) should be viewed broadly to include:

...race, religion and spirituality, age, class, culture, disability, ethnicity, gender identity, gender expression, sex and sexual orientation, immigration status and national origin.

Doing so expands awareness of potential discrimination and subtly oppressive behavior, even by well-intentioned majority group members. [1]

There is a rich literature on inter-racial and inter-cultural communication's impact on groups and organizations. (For an overview, you might examine: *Interracial Communication: Theory Into Practice* 3rd Edition by Orbe and Harris, 2013.) Diving deeply into this literature is well beyond the scope of this volume. So, here, I will only summarize some key points from just two of the many, rich and practical resources now available, on-line.

Brown University's *Diversity and Inclusion Toolkit* (https://www.brown.edu/about/administration/institutional-diversity/resources-initiatives/resources-students-faculty-staff-and-alumni/diversity-and-inclusion-toolkit) provides recommendations for fostering a welcoming, inclusive group or organizational environment. Below, are slightly modified versions of several of these recommendations, along with suggestions for their implementation. I've also incorporated some guidelines from the *Respect Ability* website (https://www.respectability.org/inclusive-philanthropy/how-to-include-people-with-disabilities/) regarding how to successfully involve individuals with disabilities. The recommendations are brief. For more detail, please access the two websites.

This is not easy work. Patterns of discrimination and oppression are so deeply baked into our society that they are often difficult to recognize and discuss, much less overcome. Yet, it is work that we are obligated to undertake, if we truly wish to promote humane groups and organizations. To do so effectively, necessarily involves occasionally setting aside some group time to frankly discuss how well your group is doing at accomplishing its goals while creating an inclusive environment. At times, it may be beneficial to hold a retreat, bringing in an outside consultant to facilitate. However, conducted, these *group processing* sessions may be awkward at first; but if conscientiously and sincerely pursued, trust will likely develop, making frank confrontation and resolution of conflicts possible.

Five recommendations are organized, below, according to the acronym, BASIC, as suggested by my colleague, Leslie Williams (2021) from Teachers College at Columbia University.

1. **B**uild an Inclusive, Respectful Team.
2. **A**ttend to the preferences of LGBTQ+ Individuals.
3. **S**upport Individuals with Disabilities.
4. **I**mplement strategies for Communicating Across Cultures.
5. **C**reate a Culture of Diversity and Inclusion.

The remainder of this section contains suggestions for promoting the humane implementation of each recommendation. While the total list of suggestions is overwhelming, it provides a helpful set of behavioral criteria for reflecting on group culture. Don't feel that you have to do everything at once or follow any specific order. Whether you are leading a business or non-profit agency, a school or college department, a volunteer or religious group, or a committee of any type; periodic review of these criteria, followed by appropriate action on one or two, can assist you in gradually creating a more welcoming environment that increases group satisfaction and performance.

1. Build an Inclusive, Respectful Team

- Develop a brief statement to share with your group about how you will work with each other, including behavioral expectations consistent with developing trust, openness, and inclusion. Such expectations might include being open to feedback rather than being defensive, respecting colleagues regardless of different styles or beliefs, and offering criticism in a constructive manner.
- Communicate concisely and regularly with colleagues regarding why an inclusive culture is important for enhancing productivity, improving communication, boosting problem solving, and fostering retention. This might include a brief review at periodic meetings, as well as a statement in all appointment letters.
- Mentor individuals in a way that clearly models desirable behaviors, not allowing intolerant behavior to go unaddressed and responding efficiently and respectfully to behaviors that mock, shame, or insult group members or others.
- Set clear expectations regarding verbal and non-verbal communication during meetings, such as no eye rolling or talking over others when disagreeing with them.
- Schedule one or two meetings a year to discuss the work environment, assess the climate, and solicit feedback about possible paths to improvement.
- Provide feedback to colleagues who need mentoring and support on improving their behavior and reinforce respectful behavior when you see it.

- Respectfully manage conflicts and disagreements in a timely and confidential manner.

2. Address the Preferences of Lesbian, Gay, Bisexual, Transgender, Queer, Plus (LGBTQ+) Individuals.

- Respectfully ask group members their preferred pronouns (e.g. they/their, she/her, she/they/their, he/his, he/they/their etc.) Be sure not to assume heterosexuality when sending invitations for meetings or events, avoiding gendered terms like Mr., Mrs., Ms, etc.
- Respond to inappropriate jokes or comments immediately, as silence sends a message of agreement.
- Do not make generalizations about any group or identity, or reveal a person's sexual orientation or gender identity, without their expressed permission.

3. Support Individuals with Disabilities

- Treat adults with disabilities as adults. Child talk is not appropriate.
- Speak directly to people with disabilities, not at their aide or sign language interpreter. Talk at eye level; if necessary, sitting in a chair to be on the same level as a person who uses a wheelchair.
- Listen patiently and attentively to a person who has difficulty speaking; do not try to finish their thoughts for them.
- Remember that a person's mobility equipment is part of their personal space. Don't move a wheelchair, cane, or scooter without their permission.

- Recognize that not all disabilities are visible or apparent, but this does not make them any less real.
- If you are unsure how to interact with a person with disabilities, ask them.
- Avoid ableism, "the discrimination or social prejudice against people with disabilities based on the belief that typical abilities are superior. It is rooted in the assumption that disabled people require 'fixing' and defines people by their disability. Ableism might even be suggested as an example of a micro-aggression." (Hart, S. 2021)
- Where appropriate, practice the principles of Universal Design, making "all environments accessible, understood, and a pleasure to use for all people. Accessibility is incorporated into event planning by considering diverse needs and abilities. When organizing a group event consider:

1. Are all products and procedures accessible, services useful, and materials marketable to people with diverse abilities?
2. Are designs flexible and accessible to a range of individual preferences and abilities?
3. Are policies and procedures easy to understand and materials simple to use?
4. Are different models of presentation used to communicate information clearly?
5. Are potential accidents minimized due to error?
6. What is the level of physical effort needed to participate and can fatigue be reduced?
7. Are events held within appropriate spaces for everyone to be welcome?" (Hart, S., 2021)

4. Implement Strategies for Communicating Across Cultures

- Demonstrate a value for diversity, communicating respect and showing empathy.
- Display flexibility and tolerate ambiguity, while avoiding being judgmental.
- Recognize your own assumptions and explore you own unconscious biases.
- Be conscious that humor necessarily involves risks and that jokes may be misunderstood.

5. Create a Culture of Diversity and Inclusion.

- Recognize that creating a workplace culture of diversity and inclusion is an ongoing developmental process for individuals and organizations, and that all group members will benefit from such an environment.
- Encourage others to be open, flexible, and receptive of differences.
- Assume that all people are individuals, who appreciate being treated with respect regardless of their ethnicity, race, nationality, religion, gender identity and expression, generational group, socioeconomic background, and other aspects of cultural identity.

Throughout all the sections of this volume that follow, please be conscious of the fact that - while not specifically addressed - diversity, equity and inclusion considerations often come into play. To lead effectively and in a humane manner, you will have to be attentive to them.

. . .

Goals, Roles, Attraction Patterns, Interaction Patterns, Norms, and Size.

Another acronym - **G.R.A.I.N.S.**- helps me to remember six variables critical within groups. The letters stand for: **G**oals, **R**oles, **A**ttraction Patterns, **I**nteraction Patterns, **N**orms, and **S**ize.

Goals

Clear goals are critical to group and organizational success. They should be explicit and agreed upon by group members. Goal confusion and conflict over goals too often result in quagmires of futile discussions and failed attempts to implement initiatives. Except under extreme circumstances - such as emergency situations - where time and resources are limited and consequences of inaction are harsh; leaders should take the time needed to consensually develop group goals. This approach ensures both the buy-in of group members and the focus required for optimal performance.

Quakers' commitment to Meeting *unity* on decisions nicely illustrate this point. Although it may take a substantial amount of time to achieve *unity*, subsequent to doing so, there is focused momentum and commitment regarding follow-through.

This is also the case in departments within a wide range of businesses, non-profits and volunteer organizations. It is always helpful for group members to have a clear notion of where they are headed, as well as agreement about where they want to go.

Roles

In addition to having clear, agreed upon goals, members of effectively performing groups and organizations need to successfully fulfill two important types of roles: **task** and **relationship.** Striking the proper balance between task and relationship behaviors is a classic leadership challenge. Ideally, leaders facilitate the distribution of task and relationship roles among group members, rather than assuming too much responsibility themselves.

Some of the specific behaviors associated with **task requirements** are:

- **Setting agendas,**
- **Maintaining focus on time,**
- **Making assignments,**
- **Giving orders,**
- **Making technical contributions,** and
- **Judging quality of products and efforts.**

Clearly, fulfilling each of these behaviors is important, but imagine how dreary life would be if they were the only foci of group and organizational activity. It would be robot-like and unbearable. Consequently, effective leadership necessarily demands the integration of a healthy dose of **relationship behaviors**, which include:

- **Seeking other's opinions,**
- **Ensuring participation by all,**
- **Offering encouragement,**
- **Mediating disputes,**
- **Celebrating successes,**
- **Inserting humor,** and
- **Providing constructive feedback.**

Again, when you consider the challenges of meeting all the requirements associated with the task and relationship demands confronting groups, it is apparent that they constitute more than one person can handle. Thus, although the designated leader may take on several of these behaviors by him or herself, encouraging shared leadership by group members in certain areas is wise. This certainly is the case in an unprogrammed Quaker meeting, where the Meeting shares the work and regularly rotates responsibilities, so tasks do not become too burdensome for any individual for too long. Of course, Meeting life may be both enriched and complicated by the fact that in larger meetings there is a substantial committee structure, with each committee having its own clerk or co-clerks and leadership effectiveness likely varying across the different committees. This variability is one of the reasons why explicit discussions of leadership skills might be valuable within any Quaker meeting. Sometimes, people are thrust into leadership roles without any sort of preparation for what they are expected to do, but this can be remedied.

What is true for Quaker meetings is also true for other organizations and their sub-groups. Whether you are a teacher, school principal, museum director, insurance company manager, politician, basketball coach, youth group leader, real estate office head, factory foreman, or any other person with supervisory responsibilities; you will find yourself navigating the delicate balance between focusing on task and relationship behaviors. Finding the proper emphasis on each of the two is an ongoing leadership challenge. Relying on the people around you to serve as resources for filling both sets of needs is remarkably helpful.

Using **humor** deserves a special note, because it can either be so helpful or harmful. Humorous quips can assist in breaking tension and making group work enjoyable, as long as they are on the mark, do not dominate work time or trivialize work efforts, and don't mock or shame group members. If you are blessed with a keen sense of humor, use it judiciously. If you aren't, don't try to infuse lame efforts. You can always allow others to provide humorous interventions. Also, never use humor to demean someone else, as it will undermine trust within your group. On the other hand, occasionally mocking yourself can set a nice tone, as self- deprecating humor can put others at ease. Finally, while approvingly acknowledging others' humorous comments, gently strive to prevent them from dominating conversation and derailing the work at hand.

Attraction Patterns, Interaction Patterns, and Norms

Groups invariably display distinct attraction patterns. People like and dislike each other to varying degrees, and these positive and negative associations play themselves out in the ways we interact with each other. While no leader should be held responsible for who likes and dislikes each other within a group, effective leaders can sometimes enhance **positive attraction** among group members by facilitating group successes. This can mean initially tackling less challenging tasks, while assuming increasingly difficult tasks over time. It almost always means fostering **interaction patterns** where all group members have opportunities to contribute and a few are not permitted to dominate the group's "air time." To do so requires establishing the right kinds of **norms,** the unwritten guidelines for group behavior, based on openness, equity and expectations of success. This is how synergies can be obtained that draw out individual strengths and fuel dynamic group performance.

When attraction and interaction patterns solidify in counterproductive ways, they work against group or organizational success. It's the leader's responsibility to prevent this from happening by continually working towards goals that are rewarding and energizing; and doing so by drawing on the emergent leadership provided by all of the group members in the areas of their greatest strengths.

In spite of Friends' good intentions and commitment to looking to "the Light" within each individual, there will always be coalitions within Quaker meetings based on naturally occurring attraction patterns. People are inclined to interact with those they perceive to be most similar to themselves, and to maintain a distance from those they perceive as "different." This can sometimes lead to awkward situations where people use loving language to cloak hostile feelings. After all, Quakers are not beyond hypocrisy. Human frailty is human frailty, among Quakers and among all other groups. As Thomas Harris (2004) argued in *I'm Ok, You're Ok,* a parent, adult and child reside within each of us, and sometimes we will have "crossed transactions," as our internal child is confronted by someone else's parent or vice versa. Anyone assuming a leadership role in a group should be prepared for these sorts of conflicts, and ready to apply the communication skills introduced in the previous chapter - active listening, I-messages and Win-Win problem solving - in order to address them.

Size

A group's size can play a critical role in its overall performance. If a group is too small (only 3 or 4 people) it may not have the task and relationship resources necessary to complete essential tasks. Furthermore, groups of three may be especially likely to encounter difficulties because two of the three members may affiliate more strongly with each other than with the third member, resulting in the third individual feeling like the "odd person out" or the "third wheel."

On the other hand, if a group is too large (a dozen or more), it may be difficult to coordinate activities, causing valuable resources to be wasted. Indeed, as group size increases, people may not speak up because they may feel that their contributions are redundant with those already posed by others. Meanwhile, a few individuals may dominate discussions. A preferable alternative is to construct teams of 6 or 7 members in order to increase the resources available to the group, while still allowing sufficient "air time" for all to make their contributions heard. Thus, the leader's responsibilities for facilitating fluid discussion incorporating the contributions of many, while keeping the group focused on the tasks at hand, can be enhanced.

. . .

Orientation, Evaluation and Control

A substantial body of small group research has demonstrated that work groups progress through phases focused on orientation, evaluation, and control. (Hare, 1976) The **orientation** phase involves obtaining clarity regarding the group's identity and purpose. This is where goal clarity (such as setting priorities or focusing on solving a particular problem) is especially important, as initial confusion can lead to prolonged, circular discussions and substantial frustration. The **evaluation** phase involves group members expressing their thoughts, opinions and feelings regarding the accuracy and merits of their goals. The **control** phase involves generating and selecting solutions to whatever matters are being addressed.

Problems may occur when leaders attempt to urge groups to take action on control measures (proposed solutions) prior to fulfilling their groups' orientation and evaluation needs. Some group members are likely to feel railroaded into doing what the leader, or other dominant group members, want. Resistance is likely to emerge, either passively or aggressively.

Within Quaker meetings, any time that a clerk attempts to prematurely close off an important discussion in order to "efficiently" move through an agenda, such resistance is likely to be palpable, due to well-ingrained assumptions about the nature of Quaker decision-making processes. However, within secular work groups, especially where there is a clear power differential between the leader and other group members, individuals may remain quiet rather than risking a rebuke by the person "in charge." Ultimately, passive aggressive behaviors among group members may result.

Matters are further complicated by the fact that any statement made by any group member during all three of the orientation evaluation and control phases may provoke **mini-phases** of orientation, evaluation and control behaviors. For example, various triggering comments may occur at any phase in a problem-solving discussion. For example: "Exactly what do you mean?"(orientation); "I can't agree with that?"(evaluation); and "We should look at it this way?" (control.)

The myriad ways that group focus and momentum can unravel illustrate the benefits of the Quaker approach of patiently seeking *unity* before acting on any substantial business item. A wise clerk recognizes this and seeks no solution before many angles of an issue have been examined and a wide array of solutions vetted. When "clarity" is finally achieved, especially on very "weighty" matters, the resulting unity in purpose results in impressive commitment to follow-through.

Similarly, secular work groups are likely to function far more effectively if they are able to achieve consensus on their perceptions of problems and their decisions to act. Whether it is a non-profit or corporate work team, clarity of purpose accompanied by unity of action dramatically increase chances of success.

Stages of Group Development: Forming, Storming, Norming, Performing, Mourning

Small task-oriented groups proceed through fairly predictable development phases. Tuchman (1965) labeled these phases: forming, storming, norming, performing and mourning. It is helpful for leaders to be able to recognize these different stages in order to promote group success.

Forming is the initial orientation phase addressed in the previous section. If group members do not become adequately oriented to each other and to the tasks that they must perform, challenges will arise that can prevent the successful progression to effective performance.

Storming is the conflict stage when group members work through their differences with each other, as well as their different opinions about their tasks and how they should be accomplished. Ineffective groups never really successfully navigate these problems. Successful groups, on the other hand, are able to engage in **norming,** which involves developing explicitly and implicitly agreed upon rules for working together. (Note: Quaker insistence on achieving "unity" within the Meeting prior to acting on decisions is a long-established norm that fosters effective action. However, the process of achieving unity can be maddeningly slow, and may not even occur. Schisms among Quakers can be devastating. For example, see Larry Ingle's *Quakers in Conflict.*) If productive norms are agreed upon, the group is more likely to proceed to the **performing** stage and achieve its peak productivity.

Finally, since the life of many groups is time-limited, there is a termination phase, which Tuchman referred to as the **mourning** stage. Even when a group stays mostly intact, it may mourn the loss of certain members who, for whatever reason, move on. Acknowledging these individuals' contributions and celebrating group successes are important activities that leaders can initiate.

One illustration is provided by my wife, Diane, and I having clerked the Memorial Committee at Hartford (CT) Monthly Meeting for many years. As clerks, we planned and facilitated memorial services with the families of recently departed friends. These services are important healing events for those of us who remain following a Friend's death. They involve both celebration and grieving for everyone. They are important punctuation marks in the history of the Meeting, significant milestones in our history.

A less dramatic example is provided by the desire/need of a successful capital campaign committee to celebrate its achievement at the close of the campaign. A public celebration may be warranted, or perhaps a small party (perhaps a pot-luck supper) just for the committee members.

Because so much of a Quaker Meeting's work is conducted by committees, which have some personnel rotating in and out every year, all committee clerks should be aware of the group development phases and the team building processes necessary to ensure that effective development takes place. This may mean starting each year with simple activities in which all committee members introduce themselves and share their expectations regarding the upcoming year's work. As always, the clerk should practice and model the communications skills described earlier in this volume in order to promote effective collaboration and, where necessary, conflict resolution.

Groupthink and Risky Shifts

One of the dangers of working with small groups, especially groups where members similar views positively reinforce each other, is becoming isolated from the world beyond the group and disparaging the views of outsiders. Social psychologist Irving Janis (1971) labeled this phenomenon **groupthink**, and warned of its consequences, including ignoring well-conceived alternatives that never get vetted. A classic illustration of this was the way that Lyndon Johnson and his immediate circle of advisers trod the path to deeper U. S. involvement in the Vietnam War, but much more mundane examples crop up in everyday life. Within schools, churches, businesses and non-profits, clusters of *insiders* with decision-making power can gradually seal themselves off from others and steer their organizations in counter-productive directions. This is especially true if group members do not feel comfortable challenging leaders' opinions.

Sometimes these decisions can lead to ***risky shifts***, involving adopting overly bold, perilous strategies. Getting caught up in the sense of invulnerability accompanying groupthink may lead group members to recklessly rush to judgement, casting aside prudent approaches. This is certainly applicable to groups of adolescents convincing themselves that they won't get in trouble for ridiculous pranks or petty crimes, but the same phenomenon is also prevalent among adults. Think of all the bad business decisions (e.g. over-investing in sub-prime mortgages) made during economic bubbles and you'll get the idea. Poor risk assessment is a common human failing and groupthink can dramatically foster it.

To prevent groupthink and risky shifts, group members should be invited to reflect critically on their efforts. This necessarily involves establishing an atmosphere of trust, so people feel secure in offering challenges to prevailing opinions. It can involve having someone play the role of devil's advocate, and taking that person's criticisms and suggestions seriously. It may even be beneficial to invite outsiders in to hear your group's plans in order to get completely different perspectives.

Even though they typically rely on prudent, consensus-oriented decision-making approaches, Quakers are not immune from risky shifts. The "sense of the Meeting" is dictated by who happens to be in attendance during the discernment and who happens to be clerking the Meeting. For example, high risk financial decisions may be made on the assumption that "Way will open." Often it does, sometimes it doesn't, and there are substantial consequences. For example, prior to some major recessions several notable Quaker organizations expanded their operations well beyond what they were able to sustain. When hard times hit, much too their consternation, they had to cut staff and programs.

---

1. For example, while Quakers can be justifiably proud of their early commitment to slavery's abolition and to their tradition of supporting oppressed minorities, Friends have demonstrated structural racism and patterns of oppression, often unaware of our actions because of our good intentions. (For a thorough analysis please see: *Fit for Freedom, Not for Friendship: Quakers, African Americans, and the Myth of Racial Justice* by Donna McDaniel and Vanessa D. Julye, 2018.)

Chapter 3

Additional Leadership Theories

"There is nothing so practical as a good theory."
Kurt Lewin

This volume started with an overview of Servant Leadership, Robert Greenleaf's theory of leadership effectiveness. You may or may not be someone who finds leadership theories helpful. Since I have benefitted from reflecting on and applying various theoretical perspectives, I am including a few here.

There are a substantial number of leadership theories; many of which are nicely summarized in books such as Northouse's (2015) *Leadership: Theory and Practice.* Three that I have found to be particularly useful are shared below. At any given time, they may provide you with guidance as you navigate group and organizational efforts.

Social Exchange Theory

> *"Social behavior is an exchange of goods, material goods but also non-material ones, such as the symbols of approval or prestige."* George Homans

In his book, *Social Behavior: It's Elementary Forms* (2nd *Ed.*), social psychologist George Homans offered six propositions underlying many of the human interactions that we engage in every day. Homans' analysis is part of a theoretical orientation known as social exchange theory.

If you carefully read the propositions, listed below, you'll see that they are interconnected and that they emphasize how individuals seek the rewards (and avoid the punishments) that they have been conditioned to see as available to them (Propositions 1&2). This plays itself out in complicated ways because people value different rewards to different degrees (Proposition 3), and rewards can lose their value over time (Proposition 4.) Also, people are likely to differ greatly in their perceptions of the likelihood of achieving the rewards that they desire (Proposition 6.) Therefore, their decisions may not always seem rational to others.

The Aggression–Approval Proposition (5a & 5b) is particularly important because it explains how people may become frustrated and angry with each other. Quite often, we expect to receive rewards which are subsequently denied us. This causes conflict with the person or people that we perceive as denying us what is rightfully ours (Proposition 5a.) The communication skills that I addressed earlier (Active Listening, I-Messages, and Win-Win Problem Solving) are all designed to help prevent or alleviate this sort of conflict, and to help individuals reach a point where they are able to work out manageable solutions and view each other favorably (Proposition 5b.) The skills are imperfect tools that may not always work, especially if clumsily applied. However, when sincerely and skillfully put to use, they can be remarkably helpful in obtaining mutually satisfying outcomes, or in understanding where things have gone wrong.

. . .

General Propositions Regarding Social Behavior

1. The Success Proposition: For all actions taken by persons, the more often a particular action of a person is rewarded, the more likely the person is to perform that action.

2. The Stimulus Proposition: If in the past the occurrence of a particular stimulus, or set of stimuli has been the occasion on which a person's action has been rewarded, then the more similar the present stimuli are to the past ones, the more likely the person is to perform the action, or some similar action, now.

3. The Value Proposition: The more valuable to a person is the result of his action, the more likely he is to perform the action.

4. The Deprivation-Satiation Proposition: The more often in the recent past a person has received a particular reward, the less valuable any further unit of that reward becomes for him.

5. **The Aggression-Approval Proposition**:

- When a person's action does not receive a reward he expected, or receives punishment he did not expect, he will be angry; he becomes more likely to perform aggressive behavior, and the results of such behavior become more valuable to him.
- When a person's action receives a reward he expected, especially a greater reward than he expected, or does not receive punishment he expected, he will be pleased; he

becomes more likely to perform approving behavior, and the results of such behavior become more valuable to him.

6. The Rationality Proposition

In choosing between alternative actions, a person will choose that one for which, as perceived by him at the time, the value of the result multiplied by the probability of getting the result, is the greater. Thus:

Action = (Probability) (Value)

The implications of these propositions for leadership are substantial. Successful leaders facilitate the acquisition of rewards for their groups. These rewards can be as varied as material goods, money, camaraderie, or sense of spiritual community. Conflicts will inevitably occur when group members differ over the rewards that should be pursued and how they should be sought. An effective leader will assist in resolving these conflicts by helping group members to achieve consensus regarding their goals and how to achieve them. Clearly, this is challenging work. Leadership is not easy. As discussed earlier, the communication skills are essential ingredients in resolving all disagreements.

The following case study illustrates how awareness of Homan's propositions might assist a Friends Meeting clerk in understanding, and subsequently facilitating resolution, of an unexpected conflict.

Case Study: The Rejected Donation

Quakers see themselves as peaceful people who persistently seek "unity" regarding key decisions confronting their meetings. Such perceptions make it especially frustrating when agreement is not easily reached. One such case involved the very well-intentioned donation of funds to a monthly Meeting for an expensive renovation project, the installation of solar panels, which the donors suggested should be conducted in a certain manner. The donors (consistent with Homans' proposition 5a) fully expected the members of the Meeting to express gratitude for the valuable gift. Instead, they were confronted with resistance from several Meeting members who believed that the donors were bypassing traditional Friends' decision-making process in order to "buy" their own preferred solution.

This situation did not allow for resolution in a single business meeting, and hard feelings persisted over a period of months. Nevertheless, through sustained efforts involving careful listening, sharing and working towards win-win solutions, the gift was returned; feelings softened; and an alternative means of funding the project was obtained. Soon afterwards, one of the donors rose to an important leadership position within the Meeting.

Situational Leadership

"Situational variables can exert powerful influences over human behavior, more... (than)... we recognize or acknowledge." Philip Zimbardo

Hersey and Blanchard's (2012) Situational Leadership Theory is an intuitively appealing leadership model. It provides a clear set of recommendations regarding how a leader should approach guiding individuals and groups under differing circumstances. There are three key variables in the model; the goal-oriented, task behavior exhibited by the leader, the leader's relationship behavior with group members, and the developmental level of the followers (how prepared they are to do the work confronting them.)

Graphically, these variables are plotted out as shown in the following table.

SITUATIONAL LEADERSHIP

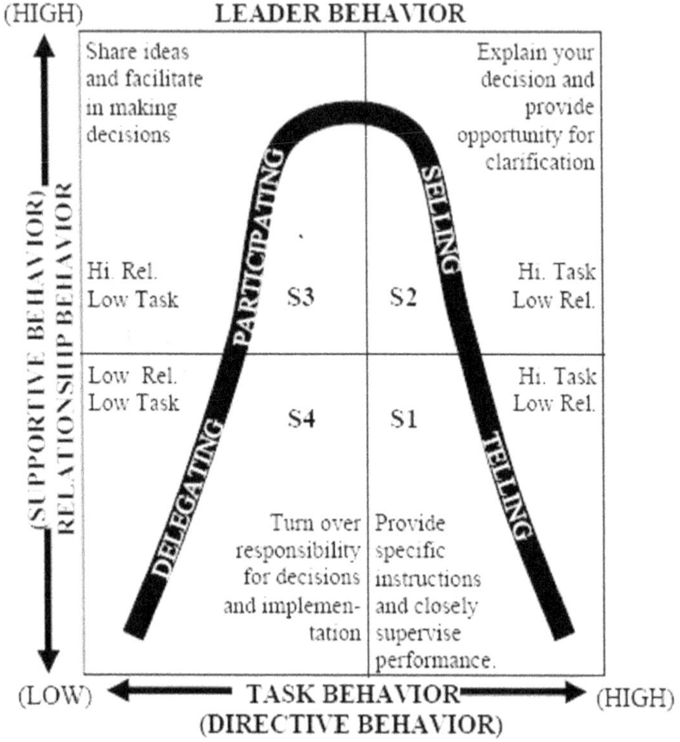

FOLLOWER READINESS

HIGH	MODERATE		LOW
R4	R3	R2	R1
Able & Willing or Confident	Able but Unwilling or Insecure	Unable but willing or Confident	Unable & Unwilling or Insecure

Source: Situational Leadership**:** A Summary Developed by Paul Hersey and Kenneth H. Blanchard. https://com-peds-pulmonary.sites.medinfo.ufl.edu/files/2014/01/Hanke-Situational-Leadership.pdf

The basic premise of the model is that a leader starts with a very directive posture, meaning a high task orientation with a low emphasis on relationships. This assumes that the followers have a low developmental level. In other words, they are not yet fully willing or capable of performing the tasks at hand. As the followers become increasingly knowledgeable regarding what is expected of them, the leader engages in increasingly more supportive, relationship-oriented behaviors, while still maintaining a high focus on task related behaviors. As follower skills further develop, the leader begins shifting to a substantially greater focus on relationship behavior, beginning to act as more of a colleague than a supervisor. Finally, as followers become capable of taking full responsibility for the work at hand, the leader can fully delegate responsibilities to the followers. If conditions warrant, and the followers are presented with demands that are overly challenging for them, the leader may return to more directive behaviors; however, the leader should not remain overly directive for too long, as a primary leadership goal is to fully develop the skills of the followers so they are not dependent on leadership from above. This whole scheme is nicely illustrated by the prescriptive curve presented above.

I've only presented the briefest description of Situational Leadership Theory, here. In order to have a much richer appreciation for Hershey and Blanchard's approach, examine the relevant materials referenced at the end of this volume, or go online and review the many articles addressing their work.

Situational Leadership Case Study: The Young Friends' First Day School Project

As part of their First Day School curriculum, a Meeting's teenage, Young Friends group conducted a community service project each year. Since all of the members of the previous year's class graduated from high school and left the area, a new younger group, composed of six, rising 9th grade students, now constituted the class. The group's two teachers were dedicated to allowing the class a substantial amount of latitude in the selection and implementation of the service project, but they realized that their time together was limited and not everyone could be counted on to show up each week. Also, the age and maturity of the group's four girls and two boys would likely lead to substantial floundering around prior to accomplishing anything substantial. Thus, they chose to be quite directive **(telling)** in their early meetings, stipulating that the group, under the teachers' close guidance: formulate a set of project goals; brainstorm a list of potential projects to meet the goals; obtain unity on a single project; and assign tasks to all six class members. Throughout, the teachers maintained visibly, enthusiastic encouragement **(selling.)**

Within a month, the class chose to serve meals at a local homeless shelter. The teachers **participated** in serving meals at the shelter and increasingly shared greater responsibility with the class in making decisions about the directions the project should take. Around Thanksgiving, the Young Friends chose to run a Christmas donation drive; collecting gloves, hats and warm socks for shelter users.

One girl in particular gradually emerged as a leader. She demonstrated great sensitivity when soliciting and listening to group members' suggestions, and she always sought unity in decision-making. Consequently, the teachers **(delegating)** urged her to encourage the group to consider other activities that they might take on during the remainder of the year and beyond. Taking up the challenge, she began conducting Skyped online, mid-week meetings exploring longer-range options. Although one class member dropped out due to her lack of commitment to the group's social activities, the other five remained highly enthusiastic and proud of their accomplishments. Ultimately, they decided to request that, over the summer, the Meeting develop a community garden spot and donate the produce to the homeless shelter. The class subsequently presented their proposal during Business Meeting, and the Meeting adopted the plan. Throughout the following summer, several adult members joined the students in cultivating the garden and transporting the produce to the shelter.

. . .

Catalytic Leadership

"Catalytic Leaders engage and motivate others to take on leadership roles and work toward a shared vision." - The Luke Center for Catalytic Leadership

The third leadership perspective is Jeffrey Luke's (1997) Catalytic Leadership, which focuses on the leadership skills necessary to resolve complex social problems. Unlike all of the previous lessons in this book, which have focused on single small groups, Luke's approach addresses the challenges confronting coalitions of groups confronting thorny, seemingly intractable issues.

Luke recognized that most difficult social dilemmas require the collaboration of multiple groups working within and across communities. He recognized that out of such collaboration can come great synergies and he developed Catalytic Leadership Theory in order to provide guidance to those committed to successfully addressing problems such as teen pregnancy, drug addiction, disease epidemics and environmental degradation. Of course, all of the lessons previously addressed in this volume are applicable within the Catalytic Leadership framework.

The seven aspects of Catalytic Leadership are:

1. **Raising Awareness**
2. **Forming Work Groups**
3. **Creating Strategies**
4. **Sustaining Action**
5. **Thinking and Acting Strategically**
6. **Facilitating Productive Work Groups**
7. **Leading from Passion and Strength of Character**

Raising awareness involves focusing public attention on an issue. Too often, communities are not aware of the severity of a problem in their own midst, much less conscious of the fact that it may be shared by surrounding communities. In such cases, ignorance is not bliss; rather it is a precondition for matters growing worse. The first step to an eventual solution is shining a spotlight on the problem, and keeping it there so the problem cannot be easily denied.

Forming working groups entails bringing individuals together to creatively address the challenges confronting them. Doing so requires patience, persistence and substantial energy. In order for working groups to persist and succeed they must consist of individuals committed to seeking long-term solutions, as well as immediate successes.

Creating Strategies is the critical stage between identifying problems and taking action steps to solve them. This necessarily involves substantial discussion regarding group members' perceptions of the problems as well as their feelings about them. Ineffective working groups are never able to satisfactorily get beyond these preliminary discussions. Successful groups navigate these discussions and are able to generate a range of action strategies, select the best from among them, and move forward. Out of these strategies, there must emerge **a shared vision** of what the participants are trying to accomplish and how they are planning to do so

Sustaining Action is essential, as working groups are always in danger of losing their momentum, especially when they consist of volunteers. People have so many competing demands on their time that their initial enthusiasm for any project, no matter how important, is likely to diminish as they get worn down by trying to fulfill their many commitments. Furthermore, they may become attracted to new causes, while still trying to address family, health and financial needs, as well as maintaining some sort of life balance. Consequently, it is crucial that work groups demonstrate progress via initial successes and, to as great a degree as possible, follow up with further successes. Setbacks are often inevitable, so flexibility and willingness to reconsider actions and regroup are vital. A group's **vision** may need to evolve in the face of complex realities. In particular, leaders should beware of falling into the arrogant trap of believing that their initial vision is necessarily the only way to proceed.

Thinking and Acting Strategically is necessary for accomplishing longer-term successes. Merely reacting to immediate challenges on a regular basis is likely to frustrate group members, causing them to question whether or not they are making the best use of their time. Similarly, to attract additional allies it is important to show a track record of substantial gains. Time must be reserved for strategic planning, but planning must not become an end unto itself. Implementation and planning must be tied together synergistically, like breathing out and breathing in.

Facilitating Productive Work Groups is an ongoing demand confronting leaders of successful collaborations. It's crucial that there be effective delegation of leadership responsibilities. By doing so, leaders can minimize the chance of burnout, as well as enhance the likelihood of ongoing success.

Leading from Personal Passion and Strength of Character energizes group efforts, while providing the trust necessary to maintain bonds over time in the face of ongoing challenges. It's naïve to assume that all group efforts will result in success. Hardships and setbacks necessarily arise. At times, leaders have to inspire through dogged determination that can only be fueled by deep personal commitment. Meanwhile, group members carefully watch leaders and render judgments as to whether or not they are "the real deal." Thus, leader integrity and consistency are essential ingredients to group success.

. . .

Catalytic Leadership Case Study: Joining the Inter-faith Alliance

The large, urban Friends Meeting appeared to be a natural member of the new Inter-faith Alliance forming in its region. However, the disintegration of a previous inter-faith initiative several years prior had left many in the Meeting unsure as to whether or not the Meeting's participation in a new effort was warranted. Much would depend on the leadership demonstrated by both the Meeting's clerk and the Alliance's executive director in providing evidence of clear direction and momentum.

Growing out of the tradition of the Industrial Areas Foundation, created by the late Saul Alinsky, the Alliance sought to hold area governments and businesses accountable for the delivery of essential services and opportunities to the urban poor. The executive director of this particular alliance, a woman in her early forties whose entire career had been spent as a Christian church community organizer, spear-headed the Alliance's launch. She approached 35 individual congregations, cutting across faiths and denominations from mosques to temples to churches to meetings; thereby **raising awareness** of the region's dramatic social inequities and emphasizing the potential of combining efforts in order to make "the system" work for the benefit of the poor.

Prior to extending an invitation to the Alliance director to attend the Quaker Meeting and a post-Meeting information session, the Meeting's clerk attended a few, early Alliance planning sessions. She then asked two interested Meeting members to meet, individually, with the executive director in order to present, at the next Meeting for Business, their recommendations about extending the invitation to the executive director. After both members reported their enthusiastic endorsements, the executive director visited the Meeting, which subsequently decided, at Meeting for Business, to join the Alliance.

Months later, after a total of three years of organizing and 85 listening sessions with more than 1,000 people, the Alliance's executive director and her staff distilled a set core issues and launched five campaigns, each of which had its own separate **work group.**

Regarding **education**, the alliance called for provision by the region's school districts of anti-racism training for all adults interacting with students. Concerning **housing**, the alliance targeted repeal of a state law allowing the Department of Social Services to seek repayment of state welfare. In **criminal justice** it sought passage of "clean slate" legislation, automatically expunging a person's criminal record three to five years after completing their sentence. In **healthcare**, the alliance chose to draft a law allowing reclaimed medications (such as those available from nursing homes) to be distributed to low-income patients by a charity pharmacy. Finally, regarding **gun violence**, sought local political commitments to join a national campaign placing financial pressure on gun manufacturers to invest in safer products and more accountable practices.

Sustaining this large, complex effort, which is still unfolding, will require **thinking and acting strategically**, with ongoing **creation of strategies** for each separate campaign**.** It is extraordinarily critical and challenging work**,** and the Alliance' s executive director, core staff and emerging volunteer leaders must constantly **facilitate productive work groups,** which can only be accomplished over the long haul by **leading from passion and strength of character.** All of the leadership skills previously addressed in this volume must come into play on a daily basis, at the small group level, in order to obtain larger successes over many years of work. Also, the relationship between the Friends Meeting and the Interfaith Alliance will be subject to review and reconsideration over time. Consequently, recurring cycles of all aspects of Catalytic Leadership will need to occur if a dynamic relationship is to be maintained.

Chapter 4

Ethics

> *"Management is doing things right; leadership is doing the right things."*
>
> Peter Drucker

At face value, the ethical demands of leading humanely seem simple enough. You just need to make sure that you always "do the right thing." However, doing what is "right" isn't always clear. Discerning an ethical path can be confounding. Merely living within groups often presents perplexing ethical dilemmas. Taking on leadership responsibilities brings additional ethical challenges. Decisions to initiate change complicate things even further.

As with so many other leadership trials, there are no foolproof guidelines when confronted with ethical decision-making. Fortunately, however, there are some helpful recommendations available. For example, there is a set of questions offered by Michael Rion (1989) in his book, *The Responsible Manager*. The questions are:

1. **Why is this bothering me?**
2. **Who else matters?**
3. **Is it my problem?**
4. **What is the ethical concern?**
5. **What do others think?**
6. **Am I being true to myself?**

Each is explained below.

1. Why is this bothering me?

Your first realization of an ethical dilemma may not present itself as obvious, conscious message, but rather as an uneasy feeling. You may sense it more in your gut, than in your head. But sooner or later, you will begin to sort out what is happening and why it is bothering you. Have some **clear duties** been neglected, by you or others? For example, has the clerk of a Meeting committee failed to meet his or her responsibilities by neglecting to schedule regular committee meetings, or failed to provide an agenda when the committee finally does meet? Or has someone in Meeting violated a **single ethical principal,** such as truth-telling? Has this involved a **single relationship,** or has the individual allegedly misled multiple people? Or is there a dispute where two or more people make **competing claims.** For example**,** members may differ substantially over the hiring of a contractor, with whom they have had very different previous experiences, to do work on the Meeting House.

2. Who Else Matters?

There are times when ethical dilemmas substantially affect as few as one or two people. For example, if you are the last living member of your family and you are weighing the moral considerations of whether you should be cremated or buried in a casket.

However, often there are wider circles of people who are affected by one's ethical decisions. It is important to identify others who might be impacted. For example, if a Quaker meeting is considering adopting a policy on clearly specifying its rationale for donations to other organizations, initial guidelines might unintentionally rule out some very worthy causes. Consequently, it is very important to carefully vet such considerations. Indeed, there are endless examples of others who are affected by many types of ethical dilemmas. Careful scrutiny should be given to the impact of decisions on others before pushing ahead.

3. Is it my problem?

When encountering an ethical dilemma, you may feel that you are obligated to solve it. However, the matter may fall beyond your jurisdiction, or it may be beyond your capacity to resolve. By addressing the matter, you may even make it worse. Obtaining clarity on who should be involved in seeking resolution is critically important.

For example, a college faculty member was distressed when a student who had a crush on her made a veiled threat against the faculty member's husband. The instructor sat on this information for a few days, but following a second threat, shared it with her department chair. The chair was also distressed, but spent several days mulling over the information, because the student was otherwise in "good academic and social standing," before deciding that she didn't know what to do and giving her dean a call asking for help. The dean immediately recognized that a matter such as this, where an individual's safety was potentially at risk, was not in the sole jurisdiction of academic officials, but primarily a matter for the campus police. She immediately put in a call to campus security, who then interviewed the faculty member and the chair, and subsequently visited the student, issuing a clear explanation regarding the seriousness of such threats and a stern warning against similar statements or any action against the faculty member's husband. The student subsequently apologized to the faculty member, and because the instructor did not wish to bring any further charges, the matter was dropped. The student graduated at the end of the semester, and never bothered the faculty member again.

4. What is The Ethical Concern?

Obtaining clarity on the specific type of dilemma with which you are confronted. Rion identifies six typical ethical concerns. As the case discussed immediately above illustrates, sometimes you are confronted with a *legal obligation*, and once that is clarified a course of action in a perplexing situation can become much more apparent. However, as the restorative justice case study below illustrates, responses to legal considerations may not always be straightforward.

Another ethical concern is basic *fairness*. Does a decision hold up when questions of equity are raised? This is illustrated by the Quaker Meeting's donations issue raised above in the *Who Else Matters* discussion.

Promise Keeping is yet another concern. Whenever we make commitments, we are morally obligated to keep them. By proclaiming the "Integrity" testimony, Quakers set a high bar for others to judge Friends' behavior.

Fundamental to the concept of Friendly Leadership is *doing good*. We should strive to assist others. The flip side of this tenet is that we should *avoid harming* them. However, sometimes we are confronted by circumstances where movement in any direction does not seem to offer clear alternatives for doing good and avoiding harm.

5. What do others think?

Even before you have fully clarified exactly why you are troubled by what is occurring, you may begin wondering who else is affected. Sorting this out can also be a challenge. For example, in cases of suspecting someone is lying or stealing, where does seeking others' views cross the line between legitimate inquiry and harmful gossip? Difficult decisions must sometime be made regarding who must be talked to and when. Also, confidentiality must be respected when people share delicate information.

For example, a college dean was once confronted with the responsibility of deciding whether or not a faculty member should be formally charged with classroom harassment. The student involved was vehement in his allegations. The faculty member was equally strong in his denials. During a lengthy discussion with the dean, the student offered that others in his classes had also been harassed, and that they could verify his claims. The dean solicited the names of three students, who she subsequently approached. Before doing so, she spoke with two longtime colleagues of the faculty member as to whether or not they had any reason to believe the accusations might be true. While acknowledging that the faculty member's flamboyant, charismatic teaching style might be intimidating to a student, they had never witnessed nor heard of anyone else claiming harassment or bullying. When the dean spoke with the three students, under strict assurances of confidentiality, none felt that they had been harassed nor believed that they had witnessed the faculty member harassing the student making the charges. On the basis of these five discussions, the dean chose to not pursue the case any further, and informed the student that as far as the college was concerned the case was closed. Furthermore, the dean alerted him that if he wanted to pursue the case any further he would have to do so in court. The student graduated that year, without raising any further issues. The faculty member taught for many more years without any further charges being filed.

6. Am I being true to myself?

Rion concludes with the most personal question: **Am I being**

true to myself? Again, for Quakers, the Integrity testimony comes into play. We have to live with the consequences of our choices. We may not be successful with our efforts, but we do need to know that, at the time, we were trying to do the right thing. Anything short of that may cause us to be haunted by the results, whether they or positive or negative.

Ethics Case Study: Restorative Justice

Rather than focusing on the decisions of a specific individual, this case study examines the collective choices made by a Meeting in response to an ethical challenge. The Meeting's new clerk had only assumed his responsibilities for twenty-four hours, in late June, when he received a telephone call alerting him that the Meeting House had been vandalized. Much of the dinnerware in the Meeting's lower-level kitchen and dining area had been smashed on the dining area floor, a space occupied on weekdays during the school year by a preschool. Also, fire extinguishers had been set off throughout the Meeting House, covering both the dining and upstairs worship areas and leaving a chemical dust throughout.

After ensuring that the police and the Meeting's insurance agency had been notified, and that a cleaning agency could begin the restoration, the clerk convened the first of several "called meetings" to "thresh out" how to proceed. It took a week for the first of these meetings to occur because it was necessary for the cleanup to be completed before the Meeting House could be occupied. By that time, the police had identified two juvenile brothers, living in the surrounding neighborhood, as the prime suspects. The brothers soon confessed. A court date was set many weeks in the future, providing the Meeting with time to discern its course of action.

The discussion at the well-attended, initial meeting was wide-ranging, cutting back and forth across many concerns. Throughout, the new clerk tried his best to apply the communication skills associated with effective clerking, adhering to norms of Quaker practice (e.g. beginning out of silence, maintaining respectful waiting, preventing individuals from dominating.) The descriptions below are not sequenced exactly as they occurred, but are organized to provide clear illustration of Rion's six questions.

Why is this bothering us?

There was an overwhelming sense of being violated among members of the Meeting. Friends initially could not imagine anything that their beloved Meeting had done to trigger such an action. However, as the discussion progressed Friends began wondering if they had set themselves off too much from the surrounding community, representing a bastion of white privilege, in spite of making the Meeting House available to a community preschool and use by many minority religious groups (e.g. Muslims, Buddhists, cross-dressing Christians, male gay Catholics.) Or perhaps the use of the Meeting House by such groups had provoked the vandalism. The Meeting just didn't know.

Who else matters?

It was apparent that all groups who used the Meeting House mattered. If the preschool had not been out of session because of the summer break, it would have been totally disrupted for at least a week. The many other groups using the Meeting House had to find alternative venues during the cleanup. However, the longer the Meeting discerned, the more it became clear that the two middle-school-aged brothers who had vandalized the Meeting House and their family, also mattered. In fact, the Meeting reached unity around the fact that they mattered most of all. Consequently, at the urging of a few members, in particular, the Meeting as a whole wondered if this series of events might provide an opportunity for the boys' moral growth.

Is it our problem?

The Meeting recognized that the situation was indeed its problem, but it was not initially sure about the extent of its responsibility for implementing a response, beyond turning the matter over to the police. Clarity was needed on the type of ethical concern.

What is the ethical concern?

At first blush this appeared to be a straightforward *legal matter*, but unity could not be obtained around bringing charges against the brothers, in spite of their confessions. Ongoing discussion focused on trying to make something *good* out of a bad situation and *avoiding harm* to the youths, but Friends remained uncertain regarding how to proceed.

What do others think?

Eventually, a well-respected member shared that he was aware of recent Friends' writings on the restorative justice process, and he offered to circulate pertinent readings on the Meeting's listserv. Furthermore, he offered to reach out to other Friends in the Yearly Meeting who had participated in restorative justice efforts to determine if they could provide any guidance. Finally, he and another Friend, a former high school guidance counselor, offered to meet with the judge who would be hearing the boys' case to determine if the judge would be open to pursuing a restorative justice approach. Another Friend, a law school professor, offered to help facilitate the discussions.

Are we being true to ourselves?

In many regards, this was the most important question of all. For Friends, deeply committed to forgiveness and "seeing what love can do," mere retribution was simply unacceptable. Finding an alternative path to harsh sentencing was imperative. In spite of having no prior experience with restorative justice, the Meeting took the plunge, hoping that *Way was opening*.

Ultimately, there were several called meetings, closely aligned with unfolding, events. The judge was open to implementing a restorative justice approach. The brothers' family also quickly agreed. A plan was devised whereby, over 18 months, the brothers would participate in the Meeting's monthly potluck lunches, following Meeting for Worship. At the potlucks, in addition to sharing the meal, the boys would help with setting up the dining area, serving the meal and cleaning up afterwards. They would also participate in occasional Meeting workdays, doing planting, painting, etc. These activities would not be onerous, and would provide the boys with opportunities to meet and talk to members of the Meeting, while working side-by-side. The family would pay no fines. The boys would have no criminal record.

This plan was implemented. The boys fully participated. All parties seemed satisfied. While it would be nice to report that the events launched a long supportive relationship between the boys, their family and the Meeting; there is no evidence of this, and the family eventually moved away from the area. However, while they remained on as the Meeting's neighbors, there were no further negative incidents.

Chapter 5

Final Thoughts

Putting It All Together

"It took me a lifetime."
Pablo Picasso

I began this volume by drawing parallels between *Friendly Leadership* and *Servant Leadership*, and frankly acknowledging that becoming an effective servant leader is a prolonged challenge. Indeed, developing one's leadership skills, under any circumstances, is a life-long endeavor. However, the good news is that we will always be presented with opportunities to learn; and if we come up short, we can benefit from our mistakes. So, we can always become better leaders if we are willing to try.

In spite of its brevity, this volume provides you with more than enough insights to fuel your leadership development for years to come. If you can successfully blend these lessons into your behavioral repertoire, you will become a more skillful leader. So remember:

1. Effective leadership requires adeptly communicating; which often includes **active listening**, **assertiveness (I-messages)** and **win-win problem solving.** Skillful communication not only helps you to prevent unnecessary conflict, it is also crucial to resolving challenging impasses when they arise.
2. Being alert to the **group dynamics** presented in Chapter 2 (Goals, Roles, Attraction Patterns, Interaction Patterns, Norms, Size, Orientation-Evaluation-Control phases, Group Development Stages, and Risky Shifts) is very helpful. And striking the balance between the appropriate focus on **task** behavior and the right emphasis on **relationship** behavior is one of the essential, recurring leadership challenges. Effective leadership involves an ongoing dance between offering challenge and providing support, with supportiveness playing a greater role over time. Hersey and Blanchard's **Situational Leadership Theory** lays this out as clearly as any model.
3. **Homans' six propositions** provide a powerful tool for analyzing group social exchanges. In particular, Proposition #5 explains why people become so upset when they are ambushed (unexpectedly denied rewards.) Also, remember that what - at first glance – appears to you like irrational behavior is often quite rational to those behaving in such a manner, given their expectations of success and their assignment of values to particular rewards.
4. When you find yourself in a situation where someone feels that you have ambushed them, take a deep breath and try to avoid scolding the person. Listen, listen, and listen some more; share deliberately; and seek a win-win solution.

5. You don't have to hold a management position in order to demonstrate effective leadership. **Catalytic leadership**, in particular, demonstrates how simply being in a position to pull together diverse allies, engaging in creative problem-solving, developing a shared vision, and being persistent can help people resolve difficult challenges.
6. **Ethics are crucial**. Always strive to do what is morally correct; but because the moral path is sometimes not apparent, remember that Rion's questions may help. They are:

Why is this bothering me?
Who else matters?
Is it my problem?
What is the ethical concern?
What do others think?
Am I being true to myself?

Losing your moral compass has serious consequences because group members watch leaders carefully, and ethical lapses quickly undermine the trust necessary to sustain productive groups and organizations. While leadership expectations vary across cultures and subcultures, integrity is universally valued.

May you maintain your integrity throughout your leadership journeys, wherever they take you.

Sources

The materials in this volume are drawn or adapted from:

Adams, Linda. https://www.gordontraining.com/free-workplace-articles /learning-a-new-skill-is-easier-said-than-done/ Retrieved April 18, 2019.

Adams, Michelle. https://www.gordontraining.com/leadership/improve-active-listening-avoiding-common-errors/ Retrieved April 18, 2019.

Bau, Margaret. https://www.quotemaster.org/group+dynamics Retrieved December 29, 2020.

Boredpanda.com. https://www.boredpanda.com/?s=funny+zoom+meetings Retrieved September 16, 2021.

Brown University. *Diversity and Inclusion Toolkit.* https://www.brown.edu/ about/administration/institutional-diversity/resources-initiatives/resources-students-faculty-staff-and-alumni/diversity-and-inclusion-toolkit. Retrieved October 24, 2021.

Drucker, Peter. https://www.azquotes.com/quotes/topics/moral-leadership.html Retrieved January 23, 2021.

Enfry, Adam. https://www.adamenfroy.com/zoom-alternative Retrieved September 24, 2021.

Gordon, T. *Leader Effectiveness Training*. Pedigree Books, 2001.

Guilford College Diversity Statement. https://www.guilford.edu/who-we-are/office-diversity-equity-and-inclusion Retrieved September 29, 2021.

Graustein. L. *New England Yearly Meeting's Experiment with Paying Attention, Friends Journal,* April 27, 2020.

Greenleaf, R. K. (2002). *Servant Leadership: A Journey into the Nature of Legitimate Power and Greatness* (25th anniversary ed.). New York: Paulist Press.

Hare, A. Paul. Handbook of Small Group Research. Publisher: Free Press; 2nd edition (1976)

Harris, Thomas. *I'm Ok, You're Ok.* New York: Harper Perennial; Reprint edition, July 6, 2004)

Hart, Sarah. *Personal Communication.* November 16, 2021.

Hersey, Paul and Blanchard, Kenneth. Management of Organizational Behavior (10th Edition) Pearson; (2012)

Homans, George. 1958. "Social Behavior as Exchange," *American Journal of Sociology* 63: 597-606.

Homans, G. *Social Behavior; Its Elementary Forms* (2nd Ed.) Harcourt Brace Jovanovich, 1974.

Ingle, H. Larry. *Quakers in Conflict,* Pendle Hill Publications; 2 edition (June 1997)

Janis, I. Groupthink, Psychology Today, 1971. Ziff-Davis Publishing Company

Lewin, Kurt https://www.verywellmind.com/kurt-lewin-biography-1890-1947-2795540 Retrieved January 22, 2021.

Luke, Jeffrey. *Catalytic Leadership: Strategies for an Interconnected World.* Jossey- Bass, 1997.

Luke Center for Catalytic Leadership https://www.thelukecenter.org/catalyticleadership Retrieved January 23, 2021.

Mattingly, B. Editor. *Help Increase the Peace Program Volume* (*4th Ed.*) American Friends Service Committee, 2009.

McDaniel, Donna and Julye, Vanessa. Fit for Freedom, Not for Friendship: Quakers, African Americans, and the Myth of Racial Justice QuakerPress of FGC: June 7, 2018.

Northouse, Peter G. *Leadership: Theory and Practice*, 7th Edition. Thousand Oaks, California: SAGE Publications, Inc 2015.

Orbe, Mark and Harris, Tina. Interracial Communication: Theory Into Practice 3rd Edition. Sage Publications: December 31, 2013.

Picasso, Pablo. https://www.goodreads.com/quotes/tag/mastery Retrieved February 3, 2020.

Rediehs, Laura. *Personal Communication.* March 24, 2020

Respect Ability. https://www.respectability.org/inclusive-philanthropy/how-to-include-people-with-disabilities/ Retrieved October 24, 2021.

Rion, Michael. *The Responsible Manager. San Francisco: Harper and Row, 1989.*

The Robert K. Greanleaf Center for Servant Leadership: http://www.greenleaf.org.

Tuckman, Bruce W (1965). *"Developmental sequence in small groups". Psychological Bulletin.* ***63*** (6): 384–399.

Williams, Leslie. *Personal Communication.* November 19, 2021.

Zimbardo, Philip. https://quotesgram.com/situational-quotes/ Retrieved January 23, 2021.

Appendix

Leading On Zoom

Dorsa Amir
@DorsaAmir

Zoom meeting schedule:

1-1:05— Waiting for the host to start the meeting
1:06— The group discovers virtual backgrounds
1:07—Someone really struggling with audio
1:09— "Let me try headphones"
1:10— Everyone holds up their cats
1:15-1:25— Actual meeting time
1:30— "Stay safe!"

536 1:49 PM · Mar 23, 2020

83 people are talking about this

boredpanda.com

When I started writing this volume, it never occurred to me to include a chapter focusing on Zoom group interactions. I didn't even know that Zoom existed. Although I had been involved in some teaching-related online meetings using Webex, they were occasional events hardly playing a substantial role in my life, or the lives of most others. Then, the pandemic hit and Zoom suddenly became a dominant platform in teaching, business and non-profit meetings, religious gatherings, arts performances and simple social gatherings. It was an amazing, overnight change that will continue to affect us in various ways, from now on.

There is nothing about Zoom meetings that nullifies the principles presented throughout this booklet, but the new technology has added a host of additional complications. As the reproduced, mocking tweet at the top of page 61 indicates, a Zoom meeting can easily go off the rails, if the meeting organizer doesn't take proper precautions.

Indeed, leading on Zoom has become a topic that easily deserves a manual of its own. I have yet to encounter one (and I'm certainly not the guy to write one), but there is a substantial amount of material already available on the Web that you can check out for yourself. Here, I'll briefly summarize a set of basic recommendations provided by Stanford University's IT support group at: https://uit.stanford.edu/news/zoom-effectively-discover-ways-lead-inclusive-meetings-and-participate-productively. Throughout, I'll include some insights based on my own Zoom experiences, both as a facilitator and participant, throughout the pandemic.

Recommendations for Effectively Facilitating Zoom Sessions

1) Plan ahead by identifying participants who can help you co-host, monitor the Chat, keep time, and take notes.

It's best if you can have all of this worked out before a meeting begins. In the case of recurring meetings, try to have a regular, designated note-taker, as well as individuals to serve as the time-keeper and Chat monitor. If that is not possible, rotating the responsibility according to a predetermined schedule allows you to avoid wasted time and the awkward silence when requests for volunteers don't yield immediate responses.

2) Acknowledge where participants are located and share rules of engagement; including keeping video on at all times, muting when not speaking, introducing one's self before speaking, and not engaging in extended discourse and side conversations on Chat.

Unless certain protocols are followed, Zoom meetings can easily be disrupted and they can possibly unravel. Turning the video camera off to conceal engaging in other activities, with the exception of necessary restroom visits, is generally bad practice. So, as a rule, cameras should stay on. Also, it is always best to mute when not speaking, because you can never be sure what noises (e.g. barking dogs, heavy machinery and squabbling children) might intrude. And in larger meetings, it is important to introduce yourself, at least the first time that you speak.

Finally, it is important to establish guidelines for the use of the Zoom Chat. While the meeting facilitator may want to encourage questions via Chat, it's important that the questions be concisely worded. Extended inquiries or shared opinions on Chat can become distracting and confusing for group members. Also, side chats between two or more participants should be discouraged, as those engaged in these chats are not fully participating in the larger meeting. (When warranted, such chats can be blocked by the meeting host.) If small group discussions are desired, they can be scheduled for Zoom "Break Out Rooms" during set times.

3) Ensure that all participants have equal access to all shared content such as agendas, slides, notes, references. Distribute these via email ahead of time, even

if you intend to, share items on screen. You can also post the agenda and selected items (that are not too content heavy) in Zoom Chat.

While it might be tempting to rely on Zoom's "Share Screen" feature to focus participants' attention on specific materials, it is generally best to provide participants, by email, materials requiring their review at least 24 hours ahead of time. The more extensive and complex the materials, the more important this precaution becomes. Also, there will be occasions when certain individuals must call in on their phones, without a Zoom app. They won't have access to screen viewing options, so prior distribution of visual materials becomes even more important.

It is often helpful to re-post the meeting agenda in the "Chat", where it is easily accessible. Other materials that are not too densely packed can also be shared this way, but avoid getting caught up in posting too much material. While some participants may be able to effectively review it while discussion is unfolding, others may get hopelessly lost, as "Chat" does not provide a particularly friendly reading format.

4) Ensure that participants have an equal chance to engage, by inviting people to speak up at multiple points in the meeting.

As with any group sessions, Zoom meetings are subject to domination by a few talkative individuals who can take up a disproportionate amount of group airtime. This tendency may be magnified by the tendency of some other individuals to be hesitant to speak on Zoom. Calling on different participants at evenly distributed points throughout a meeting can ensure adequate participation by all. Also, to keep those over-anxious to speak in check, it is advisable to establish a guideline of raising the animated hand in Zoom's "Reactions" section in order to request permission to speak.

While this may at times seem like an overly rigid requirement, it avoids the more troubling problem of people talking over each other.

5) Carefully select meeting activities. For example, ensure that ice-breakers and brainstorming sessions work for all participants.

Warm-up activities such a "check-ins," where individuals are able to share pressing joys or concerns, can be a good way to start a meeting, as can various other "ice-breaker" activities (many of which are available to you on the internet.) However, in larger group meetings, such activities can eat up way too much time that needs to be dedicated to work-related discussion. Consequently, unless the number of participants is small and manageable, it is best to have these activities occur in smaller, Zoom break-out groups. While everyone will not benefit from hearing from all colleagues, a smooth transition into group work can be achieved. Similarly, work efforts involving group activities such as brainstorming are best dedicated to "break-out" sessions, with summaries of group results reported back to the larger group.

6) Be mindful of participants with disabilities (visual, hearing, vocal).

Zoom's "Live Transcript" feature, which appears in the "Chat," provides a helpful way of assisting participants with hearing difficulties stay abreast of events transpiring during a meeting. Although the translator garbles some words, the transcripts are usually sufficient for the job at hand. Also, note takers can request the Live Transcript, which they can save to their own computers, to help them determine discussion details that they may have missed.

Participants with vocal disabilities can use "Chat" to submit their questions and comments. This makes it especially important to have someone monitoring "Chat."

Finally, as previously pointed out, visual materials displayed on Zoom can be difficult for participants to read and interpret. Of course, this is even a greater problem for blind participants, as well as those with other visual disabilities such as uncorrected refractive errors, cataracts, or glaucoma. To address these challenges to as great a degree as possible, visuals and charts should be distributed in advance, preferably as PDF files which can be enlarged as needed. During meetings, clear descriptive narratives should be provided, especially

Afterword

Zoom and various alternative meeting platforms (there are 13 listed on this link: https://www.adamenfroy.com/zoom-alternative) are here to stay. It's not clear to what extent we will be relying on them as the current pandemic restrictions subside, but at the very least we will increasingly be involved in "hybrid" meetings with some participants meeting face-to-face, while others "Zoom" in from home, or afar. Hybrid meetings introduce further issues, as whoever is leading the meeting, has to pay attention to both what is occurring on-screen and in-person. As the size of the meeting grows, the potential issues increase, accordingly.

Rather than trying to anticipate and address these hybrid-related challenges, and getting well beyond my depth, I'll stop here. I wish us all the very best, dealing with what the future holds.

Acknowledgments

Many thanks to Eugene Watson and Edward Glassman for initially stimulating my thinking about small group leadership; to Robert Cairns for showing me how social exchanges might be studied; and to all of the authors that I've cited for their impressive work. Thanks also to my colleagues and students in the University of Hartford Educational Leadership Program for years of thought-provoking leadership discussions; and to Walter Harrison, Diane Randall and Ted Sizer for modeling effective leadership in settings where I was able to both participate and observe. Also, thanks to my many Friends in Hartford Monthly Meeting, New England Yearly Meeting, Friends Committee on National Legislation, and Friends Association for Higher Education who have nurtured me, challenged me, and profoundly affected my insights.

Finally, thanks to Laura Redeihs, Diane Weinholtz, Nia Thomas and Philip Weinholtz for their thoughtful comments on drafts of this manuscript, and to the folks at Full Media Services for their assistance throughout the publishing process.

Author

Friendly Leadership

Donn Weinholtz is an emeritus Professor at the University of Hartford (CT). Over 29 years, he served the University in various capacities; directing the Doctoral Program in Educational Leadership, serving as dean of the University's College of Education, Nursing and Health Professions, chairing the Faculty Senate and sitting on the University's Board of Regents. He also taught graduate courses in professional ethics, statistics and research methods, as well as undergraduate courses in Leadership and American Studies.

Donn is a Quaker, active among Friends in Hartford, New England and the U.S. He has served as clerk of Hartford Monthly Meeting and on New England Yearly Meeting's Permanent Board. He was the founding editor of Friends Association for Higher Education's online publication, *Quaker Higher Education,* and has twice served as FAHE's clerk. He is currently one of New England Yearly Meeting's representatives to Friends Committee for National Legislation.

With his wife, Diane, a science teacher and school principal, he has co-facilitated many *Help Increase the Peace Program* (HIPP) trainings, including working with approximately 2,000 teachers in Rwanda, Africa. Diane and Donn are the parents of three grown children.